TAKE A LITTLE TIME

PRAYER IS THE KEY

The effectual fervent prayer of a righteous man availeth much.
James 5:16

Prayer gives you Strength and Power!

JENISE WILLIAMS

TAKE A LITTLE TIME – Prayer is the Key

Published 2016 by Shechinah Publishing

P.O. Box 22003 Newark, NJ 07101

Copyright © MMXVI by Jenise Williams

Printed in United States of America

Print ISBN: ISBN 978-0-692-71024-1

eBook Editions: Amazon Kindle

Unless otherwise indicated, all scripture quotations and daily devotion are taken from the *King James Bible* **(KJV), ESV, NIV, NLT** Copyright © 2016 public domain

DEDICATION

This book is dedicated to my Creator God the father,

the Son, the Holy Spirit, my children Dion, Jaqaysha,

(God-daughter) Sa'rai and in memory of my grandmother

Marie Hutcheson

"Evening, and morning, and at noon, will I pray, and cry
aloud: and he shall hear my voice." Psalm 55:17

PRESENTED TO

_____

ON

_____

CONTENTS

Preface……………………………………………..I

Acknowledgements……………………………………III

Introduction……………………………………….V

Daily Prayer Confession………………....…………VII

Week One ~ Commandment & Commitment…………….. 1

Week Two ~ Direction & Destiny……………………..11

Week Three ~ Persistence & Patience………………......21

Week Four ~ Vision & Victory…………………….…...31

Rejoice Evermore……………………………………..41

Afterword……………………………………………43

PREFACE

Prayer is Communion, Fellowship, and Relationship:

A dialogue through which is given divine direction and instruction. An address, invocation, or act that seeks to activate a rapport. A devout petition of worship, supplication, communication, thanksgiving, adoration or confession. A practice either individual or communal which take place in public or private. It may involve the use of words, song or complete silence. A request of guidance, assistance, confessing, transgressions (sins) or to express one's thoughts and emotions. A personal benefit for divine grace, spiritual connection, or for the sake of others. The tool to develop a personal, spiritual, and intimate relationship with the Creator.

And when you pray, do not be like the hypocrites, for they love to pray standing in the synagogues and on the street corners to be seen by others. Truly I tell you, they have received their reward in full. But when you pray, go into your room, close the door and pray to your Father, who is unseen. Then your Father, who sees what is done in secret, will reward you. And when you pray, do not keep on babbling like pagans, for they think they will be heard because of their many words. Do not be like them, for your Father knows what you need before you ask him.
Matthew 6:5-8

ACKNOWLEDGEMENTS

First and foremost, I would like to acknowledge my Lord and Savior Jesus Christ, who saved me from danger, destruction and gave me salvation and the gift of life.

To my children Dion and Jaqaysha who have given me the intestinal fortitude to be the best I can be! May this book continue the foundation and teach you the obedience of prayer.

To my siblings Elders Darlene and Frank Leak, Jason and Willette Jones, Keirstin Austin, Chelsea Rawls, and Yasin Bradley thank you for your love, support, and prayers. To my nephews Davion and Aiden, my beautiful nieces Rymia, Brennan, Londyn Kathleen, Zoe- Jenise, Morgan, and Aubrey I love you all to life.

To my biological parents Joyce Jenkins and James Wescott thank you for making the best choice of giving me life. I Love You!

To the three special women God planted into my life who represent the Trinity: Auntie-Mom Rebecca Hutcheson (Sayidda Mohammed) thank you for taking the time to teach, nurture, and groom me into the woman I have become; to my two spiritual mothers, who took on the role of God-Mother(s) Pastor (Mom) Esther Lundy and Executive Pastor (Mom) Janet Harris thank you for your wisdom, support, guidance, and Agape love! You both are the epitome of a mother.

To Pastor/Prophet Jerry C. Williams, Sr. who has been a great inspiration and encourager. He always assured me **"Failure is Not an Option!"**

In all these things we are more than conquerors through him that loved us.   *Romans 8:37*

INTRODUCTION

With the hustle and bustle of life it is imperative to be a good Steward of time! **Time** is the continued progress of existence. A component quantity of measurement used to order events from the past, through the present, into the future, which compare the duration of events and the intervals between them.

The Creator is time, he is **Kairos -** a propitious, appointed, opportune moment, supreme or due season; and **Chronos -** the personification of time, chronological or sequential order in which everything happens.

Our Creator requires you to take a little time out of your daily routine to devote to him. Time to develop intimate friendships, fellowships, courtships and relationships. *If we seek first the kingdom of God and his righteousness, all things will be added to us. Matthew 6:33*

We must pay attention and take advantage of the opportune times and seasons in our lives. *To everything there is a season, and a time to every purpose to everything under the heaven. Ecclesiastes 3:1*

A relationship with lack of communication cannot be strengthened. Take time to communicate with the Creator, He's never too busy to take time for you.

Be careful for nothing; but in everything by prayer and supplication with thanksgiving let your requests be made known unto God. And the peace of God, which passeth all understanding, shall keep your hearts and mind through Christ Jesus.

Philippians 4:6-7

V

DAILY PRAYER CONFESSION

Father, I come boldly to the throne of grace, that I may obtain Your mercy; You are my Shepherd and I shall not want; Father forgive me, I repent for sins of commission and omission; create in me a clean heart, and renew a right spirit within; thank you for Your peace which surpasses all understanding. Though I walk through the valley of the shadow of death, I will fear no evil, for thou art with me; You will never leave me nor forsake me, You hath not given me the spirit of fear, but of power, and of love, and of a sound mind. According to your word your favour goes before me, goodness and mercy shall follow me all the days of my life. Thank you for directing my path, you make every crooked place straight, rough places smooth, a way in the wilderness, rivers in the desert, thank you for filling every void. You are Elohim, the Author and Finisher of my Faith, El-Shaddai, my redeemer, thank You for Your promises; because greater is he that is in you, than he that is in the world. No weapon formed against me shall prosper, and every tongue that rises against me shall be condemned in judgment. I am **Victorious and Triumphant** over every **Test, Trial**, and **Tribulation.** As I abide in You, and Your word abides in me, whatsoever I ask it shall be done.

I seal this prayer in the **BLOOD of Jesus.** Amen

Week One

COMMANDMENT

AND

COMMITMENT

"Abide in his love commit to the commandments, ask what you will and it shall be done unto you."

John 15:7

Sunday

Morning
This is the day the LORD has made; we will rejoice and be glad in it - Psalm 118:24

Abba Father, thank You for this day I have never seen and will never see again. I decree and declare today will be one of the best days of my life; it shall be blessed and prosperous as I rejoice.

Afternoon
Trust in the Lord with all your heart, and do not lean on your own understanding. In all your ways acknowledge him, and he will make straight your path - Proverbs 3:5-6

Abba Father, I will acknowledge You. You are my compass that guides me through the path of righteousness. I do trust you with all my heart.

Evening
Peace I leave with you; my peace I give you. I do not give to you as the world gives. Do not let your hearts be troubled and do not be afraid - John 14:27

Abba Father, Thank You for giving me Shalom, peace, harmony and tranquility which surpasses all understanding in the time of need. I shall not be troubled because of my peace that You alone give unto me.

Monday

Morning
Cause me to hear thy lovingkindness in the morning; for in thee do I trust: cause me to know the way wherein I should walk; for I lift up my soul unto thee - Psalm 143:8

Abba Father My voice shalt thou hear in the morning; O LORD; in the morning will I direct my prayer to thee, and will look up to You!

Afternoon
Every good and perfect gift is from above, coming down from the Father of the heavenly lights, who does not change like shifting shadows. - James 1:17

Abba Father, I long after You and Your exceeding grace. Your word is perfect, the truth, the way and the light. Thank You for the gift of life.

Evening
Trust in the Lord forever, for the Lord, the Lord himself, is the Rock eternal - Isaiah 26:4

Abba Father, You are my rock and foundation. Your promises are eternal and I will stand firm and declare Your greatness.

Tuesday

Morning
But I cry out to you, LORD; in the morning my prayer comes before you - Psalm 88:14

Abba Father, This morning I will cry out to You. I lay my requests before you and wait expectantly for your kingdom come, your will be done, on earth as it is in heaven.

Afternoon
Commit your works to the LORD and your plans will be established - Proverbs 16:3

Abba Father, Your covenant established upon better promises, fill my heart with Your grace. Thank You for your plans to prosper and not to harm, plans to give hope and a future.

Evening
Let us therefore come boldly unto the throne of grace that we may obtain mercy, and find grace to help in the time of need - Hebrews 4:16

Abba Father, Thank You for Your help in the time of need. Your undeserved gifts of grace, favor, and love. I glorify you both now and forever.

Wednesday

Morning

My voice shalt thou hear in the morning, O LORD; in the morning will I direct my prayer unto thee, and will look up - Psalms 5:3

Abba Father, I look up to you this morning and I direct my prayer unto you. Hear my prayer, O Lord, give ear to my voice and supplications in thy faithfulness answer me, and in thy righteousness.

Afternoon

The Lord is my strength and song, and he is become my salvation: he is my God, and I will prepare him a habitation; my father's God, and I will exalt him - Exodus 15:2

Abba Father, My salvation I will trust, and not be afraid for you are my strength and my song. You are my protector and my deliverer. El Shaddai I praise You.

Evening

Be strong and of a good courage; be not afraid, neither be thou dismayed: for the Lord thy God is with thee whithersoever thou goest - Joshua 1:9

Abba Father, I will not be afraid of those that have set themselves against me, You lift up a standard. I am strong and mighty through You. Great is thy faithfulness.

Thursday

Morning
Honour the Lord, with thy substance, and with the first fruits of all thine increase - Proverbs 3:9

Abba Father, Whatsoever I do in word or deed, I give unto You my first fruits, praise and thanksgiving for another day.

Afternoon
For this is the love of God, that we keep his commandments: and his commandments are not burdensome – 1 John 5:3

Abba Father, I stand in covenant with your word to keep your commandments, which is not a burden but a delight and joy to soul.

Evening
And the peace of God, which passeth all understanding, shall keep your hearts and minds through Christ Jesus - Philippians 4:7

Abba Father, Your peace is my peace, and my peace is my power. Thou wilt keep me in perfect peace, whose mind is stayed on thee: because I trust in thee.

Friday

Morning
Teach me thy way, O LORD; I will walk in thy truth: unite my heart to fear thy name - Psalm 86:11

Abba Father, My soul thirsts for You. Thou shall teach me Thy wisdom and I will obey Thy command. You are good; your mercy; is everlasting; and your truth endures to all generations.

Afternoon
May the favor of the Lord our God rest on us; establish the work of our hands for us-yes, establish the work of our hands - Psalm 90:17

Abba Father, I decree your favor shall rest upon me according to your word. I shall eat the fruit of my labor; blessings and prosperity shall be unto me; for you have established the work of my hands.

Evening
By day the Lord commands his steadfast love, and at night his song is with me, a prayer to the God of my life – Psalm 42:8

Abba Father, I delight in You, a steadfast, abounding love. I meditate on Your laws day and night as your song is with me and quiet my soul.

Saturday

Morning
Let your heart therefore be wholly devoted to the LORD our God, to walk in His statutes and to keep His commandments, as at this day - 1 Kings 8:61

Abba Father, I keep your commandments that I may walk in Your statutes. Your spirit hath made me, and the breath of the Almighty hath given me life. Thank You for another day. I give my heart wholly to you.

Afternoon
Fear not, for I am with you; be not dismayed, for I am your God; I will strengthen you, I will help you, I will uphold you with my righteous right hand - Isaiah 41:10

Abba Father, I will not allow distress to overtake me for you re always with me. I receive your strength and Your help as Your righteous hand holds me up

Evening
The faithful God, which keepeth covenant and mercy with them that love him and keep his commandments to a thousand generations - Deuteronomy 7:9

Abba Father, I have hid Your righteousness within my heart; I will declare Your faithfulness and loving-kindness. I receive Your mercy and walk in love as I keep your commandments.

Week Two

DIRECTION

AND

DESTINY

"Oh, that you would bless me and enlarge my territory! Let your hand be with me, and keep me from harm so that I will be free from pain."

1 Chronicles 4:10

Sunday

Morning
Great is his faithfulness; his mercies begin afresh each morning - Lamentations 3:23

Abba Father, Thank You for Your fresh mercies and compassion. I receive Your grace which has been proven and failed not. I have life because you live.

Afternoon
The steps of a good man are ordered by the Lord: and he delighteth in his way - Psalm 37:23

Abba Father, my ways are directed to keep Thy statues, by this I know that You favor me. Thank You for setting my feet upon a rock, and establishing my goings.

Evening
Take my yoke upon you, and learn of me; for I am meek and lowly in heart: and ye shall find rest unto your souls - Matthew 11:29

Abba Father, I reverence You as a sovereign God. Thank You for granting access to come before You with confidence. My mind, body and soul shall be at ease to learn of you and I find rest for my spirit.

Monday

Morning
For I know the thoughts that I think toward you, saith the LORD, thoughts of peace, and not of evil, to give you an expected end – Jeremiah 29:11

Abba Father, I shall not fear now, nor the future, for Your word declares peace and promises. I give you Praise for for an expected end that you have prepare for me.

Afternoon
For the vision is yet for an appointed time, but at the end it shall speak, and not lie though it tarry, wait for it because it will surely come, it will not tarry – Habakkuk 2:3

Abba Father, I will wait for Your appointed time. Thank You for the directions and instructions to my destiny. It shall come and will not delay.

Evening
My soul yearns for you in the night; my spirit within me earnestly seeks you - Isaiah 26:9

Abba Father, As the deer panteth for the water, my soul yearns for. You are my heart's desire and my spirit earnestly seeks You. Thank You for watching over me keeping me safe from all harm.

Tuesday

Morning
I love those who love me, and those who seek me diligently find me -Proverbs 8:17

Abba Father, I shall rise early to seek Thee, that I may find You. Thank You for Your love, for Your strength, grace and faithfulness which gives me another productive day.

Afternoon
Let your light so shine before men, that they may see your good works, and glorify your Father which is in heaven - Matthew 5:16

Abba Father, Let the redeemed light the way as the Lord has said; help me to display Your glory through love, compassion, and forgiveness, that others will glorify You.

Evening
Come unto me, all ye that labour and are heavy laden, and I will give you rest -Matthew 11:28

Abba Father, Thank You for extending the invitation to release sins of omission and commission that we may rest in the gift of salvation, peace and joy.

Wednesday

Morning

The Sovereign LORD has given me a well-instructed tongue, to know the word that sustains the weary. He wakens me morning by morning, wakens my ear to listen like one being instructed - Isaiah 50:4

Abba Father, This tongue shall be your tool to speak a word to the weary. As I wake my ear listens to receive your instruction. I bring forth prayers and requests unto You and eagerly await Your guidance.

Afternoon

For thou art my rock and my fortress; therefore for thy name's sake lead me, and guide me – Psalm 31:3

Abba Father, guide me in the path of righteousness, make Your way straight before me. When storms arise You are my rock and my fortress. Bless the work of my hands so shall it be pleasing unto You, and bring praise to Thy name.

Evening

To declare your lovingkindness in the morning and your faithfulness by night – Psalm 92:2

Abba Father, May my prayers be counted as incense before You. May the lifting up of my hands as the evening offering, speak well of your faithfulness.

Thursday

Morning
My soul waits for the Lord more than the watchmen for the morning – Psalm 130:6

Abba Father, my soul eagerly awaits the gifts of Your grace and power. You are good, faithful and just. I will declare Your lovingkindness.

Afternoon
Ask, and it shall be given you; seek, and ye shall find; knock, and it shall be opened unto you - Matthew 7:7

Abba Father, this day shall be sought with humility, as I seek You. I will persevere and be diligent that my deeds be acceptable in Thy sight. I decree every door you have ordained for me shall be opened.

Evening
So shall my word be that goeth forth out of my mouth: it shall not return unto me void, but it shall accomplish that which I please, and it shall prosper in the thing whereto I sent it - Isaiah 55:11

Abba Father, Your word is a lamp unto my feet, and a light unto my path. I am thankful that it is trustworthy and does not fail. It shall prosper where you send it.

Friday

Morning
Seek the kingdom of God above all else, and live righteously, and he will give you everything you need - Matthew 6:33

Abba Father, Your word declares if I live righteously, riches and honor are with me, with enduring wealth, salvation, wisdom and knowledge.

Afternoon
Seek the LORD and his strength; seek his presence continually - 1 Chronicles 16:11

Abba Father, I shall seek You wholeheartedly. You will make known to me the path of life. You promise to reward those who diligently seek You. In Your presence is fullness of joy and in Your right hand there are pleasures forever.

Evening
The Lord is good, a strong hold in the day of trouble; and he knoweth them that trust in him - Nahum 1:7

Abba Father, I trust you with all my heart. For in the time of trouble You shall hide me in the secret of Your tabernacle and he shall set me up upon a rock.

Saturday

Morning
The day is thine, the night also is thine: thou hast prepared the light and the sun – Psalm 74:16

Abba Father, Your light gives life more abundantly. I will let my light so shine before men, that they may see your good works, and glorify the Father which is in heaven.

Afternoon
Therefore, my beloved brothers, be steadfast, immovable, always abounding in the work of the Lord, knowing that in the Lord your labor is not in vain - 1 Corinthians 15:58

Abba Father, I shall not allow anything to shake my faith, move my hope, or change my belief; not for any time. I am fully persuaded that my labor is not in vain.

Evening
Bless the Lord, O my soul, and all that is within me, bless his holy name – Psalm 103:1

Abba Father, May my praise and meditation be pleasing unto You. Thank You for sweet sleep, I shall arise rested and strengthen ready to bless and extol Your name.

Week Three

PERSISTENCE

AND

PATIENCE

My heart rejoices in the Lord; in the Lord my horn is lifted high. My mouth boasts over my enemies, for I delight in your deliverance. "There is no one holy like the Lord; there is no one besides you; there is no Rock like our God.

1 Samuel 2:1-2

Sunday

Morning
Let the words of my mouth, and the meditation of my heart, be acceptable in thy sight, O LORD, my strength, and my redeemer - Psalms 19:14

Abba Father, Thank You for a new day, it is Your doing; it is marvelous in our eyes. I ask that words of my mouth this day be pleasing unto You. You are my strength and you alone have redeemed me.

Afternoon
And let us not be weary in well doing: for in due season we shall reap, if we faint not - Galatians 6:9

Abba Father, I shall not allow tests, trials, or tribulations to push me to quit. I will persevere with purpose, power, and persistence. I shall not faint.

Evening
But for this purpose I have raised you up, to show you my power, so that my name may be proclaimed in all the earth - Exodus 9:16

Abba Father, thank You for Your power that I may know my purpose. I shall stand against the wiles of the adversary and proclaim the victory in Your name.

Monday

Morning
Humble yourselves, therefore, under the mighty hand of God so that at the proper time he may exalt you - 1Peter 5:6-7

Abba Father, I come to Your throne humbly and boldly. I thank You for Your grace I shall display Your glory, when you have exalted me at the proper time.

Afternoon
The end of a thing is better than its beginning; The patient in spirit is better than the proud in spirit – Ecclesiastes 7:8

Abba Father, I glory in tribulations also knowing that tribulation worketh patience. But if we hope for that we see not, then do we with patience wait for it. Patience produces faith, and the testing of my faith produces endurance.

Evening
When you lie down you will not be filled with fear; when you lie down your sleep will be pleasant – Proverbs 3:24

Abba Father, The LORD is my light and my salvation; whom shall I fear? The LORD is the strength of my life; of whom shall I be afraid? Thank You for sweet sleep. I shall awaken rested, renewed, and recharged.

Tuesday

Morning
And we know that in all things God works for the good of those who love him, who have been called according to his purpose - Romans 8:28

Abba Father, Thank You for Your irrevocable gifts and call. This is for your benefit, so that the grace that is extending may overflow in thanksgiving.

Afternoon
To everything there is a season, and a time to every purpose under the heaven -Ecclesiastes 3:1

Abba Father, Thank You for every season You have ordained for my life. You make the crooked places straight as I follow Your guidance. Fill my valley with springs of water and fill every void in my life.

Evening
For I reckon that the sufferings of this present time are not worthy to be compared with the glory which shall be revealed in us. - Romans 8:18

Abba Father, You are with me, I am not dismayed; for you will strengthen, help and uphold me with Your right hand of Your righteousness. Your glory shall be revealed.

Wednesday

Morning
O Lord, be gracious to us; we wait for you. Be our arm every morning, our salvation in the time of trouble - Isaiah 33:2

Abba Father, I shall seek You early while You may be found, I wait for you. You are Jehovah Nissi, I long for you. You are my strength every morning, my salvation in time of distress

Afternoon
For ye have need of patience, that, after ye have done the will of God, ye might receive the promise -Hebrews 10:36

Abba Father, I decree and declare victory over every trial and tribulation; my patience is composed of confidence and hope. I believe and receive every promise for my life.

Evening
The Lord is my shepherd; I shall not want. He maketh me to lie down in green pastures: he leadeth me beside the still waters – Psalm 23:1-2

Abba Father, You are my provider and protector. You lead me to abundance and there shall not be any lack. Thank you for redeeming and restoring.

Thursday

Morning
And in the morning, rising up a great while before day, he went out, and departed into a solitary place, and there prayed -Mark 1:35

Abba Father, I follow your pattern I rise and take solace and call upon, and praise Your name. You are my glory and lifter of my head.

Afternoon
Now unto him that is able to do exceeding abundantly above all that we ask or think, according to the power that worketh in us -Ephesians 3:20

Abba Father, Thank You for Your absolute power to do all things. Your power which works in me and the evidence of Your exceeding greatness will shine in my life to show forth your glory.

Evening
I have told you these things, so that in me you may have peace. In this world you will have trouble. But take heart! I have overcome the world – John 16:33

Abba Father, I take confidence in your word when trouble arise, I can rejoice in all these things. I am more than conqueror through him that loved us.

Friday

Morning
Weeping may stay for the night, but rejoicing comes in the morning - Psalm 30:5

Abba Father, Thank You for the morning. Guide me through this day. In Your presence is fullness of joy, in Your right hand there are pleasures forever. I will rejoice.

Afternoon
Many are the plans in a human heart, but it is the LORD's purpose that prevails - Proverbs 19:21

Abba Father, Cleanse me with hyssop and I will be clean; wash me and I will be whiter than snow; create in me a clean heart and renew a steadfast spirit within me. I am rejoicing with gladness for my future.

Evening
You need not fear the terrors of the night, the arrow that flies by day – Psalm 91:5

Abba Father, For we wrestle not against flesh and blood, but the darkness of this world, against spiritual wickedness in high places. I shall not fear the terrors; I have a place of refuge in my God.

Saturday

Morning
Finally, my brethren, be strong in the Lord, and in the power of his might - Ephesians 6:10

Abba Father, I can do all things through Christ that strengthens me, I am strong and courageous. For You are with me wherever I go.

Afternoon
Behold, I give unto you power to tread on serpents and scorpions, and over all the power of the enemy: and nothing shall by any means hurt you - Luke 10:19

Abba Father, No weapon that is formed against me will prosper; and every tongue that accuses in judgment You will condemn. This is the heritage of your servants.

Evening
Now may the Lord of peace himself give you peace at all times and in every way - 2 Thessalonians 3:16

Abba Father, Thank You for giving peace at all times in every way. Your countenance that gives grace, love, comfort and peace which surpasses all understanding. Guard my heart and mind, that I may take comfort in this peace that only you can give.

Week Four

VISION

AND

VICTORY

Blessed be thou, Lord God of Israel our father, for ever and ever. O Lord is the greatness, and the power, and the glory, and the victory, and the majesty: for all that is in the heaven and in the earth is thine; thine is the kingdom, O Lord, and thou art exalted as head above all. Both riches and honour come of Thee, and thou reignest over all; and in thine hand is power and might; and in thine hand it is to make great, and to give strength unto all. Now therefore, our God, we thank thee, and praise thy glorious name. **1 Chronicles 29**

Sunday

Morning
The Lord bless thee, and keep thee: The Lord make his face shine upon thee, and be gracious unto thee: The Lord lift up his countenance upon thee, and give thee peace - Numbers 6:24-26

Abba Father, Thank You for favor, for it is written, eye hath not seen, nor ear heard, neither have it entered into the heart of man the things You have prepared.

Afternoon
I press toward the mark for the prize of the high calling of God in Christ Jesus - Philippians 3:14

Abba Father, I run with a definite aim for the prize which You have ordained for my life. Your everlasting wisdom, favor and power have crowned my life.

Evening
The God of peace will soon crush Satan under your feet. The grace of our Lord Jesus be with you – Romans 16:20

Abba Father, Through Your word and power I am victorious. Your peace that surrounds me gives me the assurance that I receive your grace.

Monday

Morning
Give thanks to the LORD, for he is good; his love endures forever - 1 Chronicles 16:34

Abba Father, You are Alpha and the Omega, who is, and who was, and who is to come; my soul sing praise and give thanks to You forever.

Afternoon
God is my strength and power: and he maketh my way perfect - 2 Samuel 22:33

Abba Father, Some trust in chariots and some in horses, I trust in You. Thank You for Your guidance to a triumphant purpose. You are my rock, my fortress, and my strength. You have made my way perfect and my soul flourishes in You.

Evening
I will lie down and sleep peacefully, for you, LORD, make me safe and secure - Psalm 4:8

Abba Father, Thank You for peaceful sleep. I bind fearful dreams, and loose peace. I am secure and confidence that I abide in safety.

Tuesday

Morning
I will praise thee, O Lord, with my whole heart; I will shew forth all thy marvelous works - Psalm 9:1

Abba Father, With gratitude and adoration I thank You for this day; the blessings upon my life shall be the testimony of Your wonderful deeds.

Afternoon
But my God shall supply all your need according to his riches in glory by Christ Jesus - Philippians 4:19

Abba Father, You are the master of my need. I decree and declare abundance and overflow. I bind the spirit of poverty and loose prosperity in my life.

Evening
My eyes stay open through the watches of the night, that I may meditate on your promises – Psalm 119:148

Abba Father, I commit my way and trust in You. I cast all my cares upon You, because You care for me. In the evening I will meditate on Your promises. Your word declares your promises are yea and Amen.

Wednesday

Monday

And all these blessings shall come upon you and overtake you, if you obey the voice of the LORD your God - Deuteronomy 28:2

Abba Father, Thank You for a new day, new mercies, new opportunities. As I obey your voice the blessings You have predestined shall overtake my life exceeding abundantly.

Afternoon
Every man also to whom God hath given riches and wealth, and hath given him power to eat thereof, and to take his portion, and to rejoice in his labour; this is the gift of God – Ecclesiastes 5:19

Abba Father, Thank You for that which You given me. My fruit is better than gold, durable riches and honor are with me. I give you praise, glory, and honor for this gift.

Evening
Call to me and I will answer you and tell you great and unsearchable things you do not know - Jeremiah 33:3

Abba Father, Thank You for hearing my voice, because You inclined Your ear to me, I shall call upon You as long as I live. Thank You for victory in unsearchable things. Your revelation brightens my path.

Thursday

Morning
O Lord, how excellent is thy name in all the earth! Who hast set thy glory above the heavens - Psalm 8:11

Abba Father, I arise giving You praise for Your wonders. I am grateful for Your faithfulness, Your mighty acts, and excellent greatness., will I declare in the earth.

Afternoon
The Lord is good unto them that wait for him, to the soul that seeketh him – Lamentations 3:25

Abba Father, I shall wait upon You, thank You for renewed strength; for wings as eagles. I shall not give up; I will endure until the end.

Evening
By him therefore let us offer the sacrifice of praise to God continually, that is, the fruit of our lips giving thanks to his name – Hebrew 13:15

Abba Father, let the words of my mouth, and the meditation of my heart, be acceptable in Thy sight. You are my strength and redeemer. I offer the sacrifice of praise with the fruit of my lips, bringing glory to Your name.

Friday

Morning
You make known to me the path of life; you will fill me with joy in your presence, with eternal pleasures at your right hand - Psalm 16:11

Abba Father, Thank You for the unspeakable gift of life. I stand in your presence filled with joy. I have been endowed with eternal pleasures and with thanksgiving, I rejoice.

Afternoon
But thanks be to God! He gives us the victory through our Lord Jesus Christ - 1 Corinthians 15:57

Abba Father, I give thanks in every circumstance, for greater works shall I do in Your name, for whatsoever I ask in Your name, it shall be done. I declare my victory.

Evening
The Spirit Himself bears witness with our spirit that we are children of God – Romans 8:16

Abba Father, Thank You for the blood tie covenant. I am chosen in royal priesthood of Your holy nation, and I shall shew forth the praises unto You.

Saturday

Morning
God blesses those who are humble, for they will inherit the whole earth - Matthew 5:5

Abba Father, I awake this day filled with humility and the reverence of You. Thank You for Your instruction of wisdom, riches, honour, and life.

Afternoon
Give thanks in all circumstances; for this is the will of God in Christ Jesus for you - 1 Thessalonians 5:18

Abba Father, I enter into Your presence with thanksgiving, for You are good. Your mercy and steadfast love endures forever. You shall be praised forever.

Evening
The Lord shall open unto thee his good treasure, the heaven to give the rain unto thy land in his season, and to bless all the work of thine hand – Deuteronomy 28:12

Abba Father, Your word declares, I shall enjoy the good of my labour. It is a gift from You. Your blessings make me rich and add no sorrow. I shall be the head, and not the tail; I shall be above only, and not beneath; this is Your will.

REJOICE EVERMORE

There is no sin the Creator will not forgive.

There is no prayer the Creator will not hear.

Cast all your cares and burdens on Him,

for He cares for you

If you're ready for a new beginning

Accept this Invitation to the Father… Romans 10:9-10

If thou shalt confess with thy mouth the Lord Jesus, and shalt believe in thine heart that God hath raised Him from the dead, thou shalt be saved. For with the heart man believeth unto righteousness, and with the mouth confession is made unto salvation.

Amen

AFTERWORD

If my people, which are called by my name, shall humble themselves, and pray, and seek my face, and turn from their wicked ways; then will I hear from heaven, and will forgive their sin, and will heal their land.

2 Chronicles 7:14

Prayer is a Privilege which provide Power and Purpose.

Prayer is our supernatural **(AAA) key.**

It unlocks Access, Authority and **Ability!**

We should never go a day without it!

Take A Little Time
Prayer is the Key